EXPLORING CIV

D0562622

THE MOVEMENT

1960

SELENE CASTROVILLA

Franklin Watts®
An imprint of Scholastic Inc.

Content Consultants

Senator Nan Grogan Orrock
State of Georgia

Crystal R. Sanders, Ph.D.
Associate Professor of History
Pennsylvania State University

Library of Congress Cataloging-in-Publication Data
Names: Castrovilla, Selene, author.
Title: Exploring civil rights— the movement : 1960 / by Selene Castrovilla.
Description: First edition. | New York : Franklin Watts, an imprint of Scholastic Inc., [2022] | Series: Exploring civil rights | Includes bibliographical references and index. | Audience: Ages 10–14. | Audience: Grades 5–8.
Identifiers: LCCN 2021020381 (print) | LCCN 2021020382 (ebook) | ISBN 9781338769777 (library binding) | ISBN 9781338769784 (paperback) | ISBN 9781338769791 (ebook)
Subjects: LCSH: African Americans—Civil rights—History—Juvenile literature. | Civil rights movements—United States—History—20th century—Juvenile literature. | Civil rights workers—United States—Juvenile literature. | BISAC: JUVENILE NONFICTION / History / United States / 20th Century | JUVENILE NONFICTION / History / United States / General
Classification: LCC E185.61 .C294 2022 (print) | LCC E185.61 (ebook) | DDC 323.1196/073—dc23
LC record available at https://lccn.loc.gov/2021020381
LC ebook record available at https://lccn.loc.gov/2021020382

Copyright © 2022 by Scholastic Inc.

All rights reserved. Published by Franklin Watts, an imprint of Scholastic Inc., *Publishers since 1920.* SCHOLASTIC, FRANKLIN WATTS, and associated logos are trademarks and/or registered trademarks of Scholastic Inc.

The publisher does not have any control over and does not assume any responsibility for author or third-party websites or their content.

No part of this publication may be reproduced, stored in a retrieval system, or transmitted in any form or by any means, electronic, mechanical, photocopying, recording, or otherwise, without written permission of the publisher. For information regarding permission, write to Scholastic Inc., Attention: Permissions Department, 557 Broadway, New York, NY 10012.

10 9 8 7 6 5 4 3 2 1 22 23 24 25 26

Printed in Heshan, China 62
First edition, 2022

ON THE COVER: Students holding a sit-in to desegregate lunch counters in the South spent their time studying and reading despite not being served.

Series produced by 22MediaWorks, Inc.
President LARY ROSENBLATT
Book design by FABIA WARGIN and AMELIA LEON
Editor SUSAN ELKIN
Copy Editor LAURIE LIEB
Fact Checker BRETTE SEMBER
Photo Researcher DAVID PAUL PRODUCTIONS

PREVIOUS PAGE: Student demonstrator John Lewis (right) is photographed through the glass door as he leaves the restaurant where he and James Bevel were staging a sit-in to protest discriminatory practices.

Ax Handle riot, page 45

Table of Contents

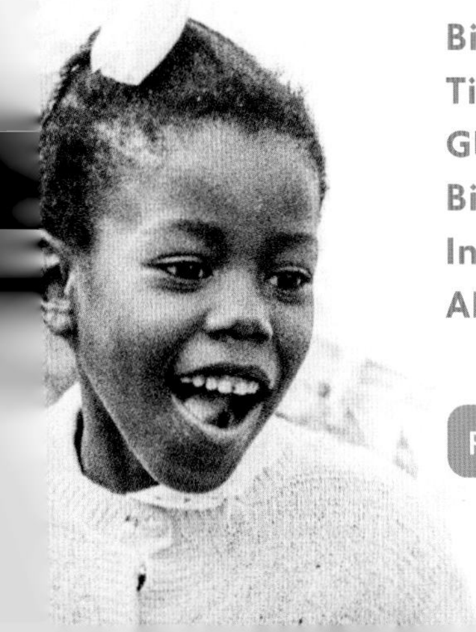

Ruby Bridges, page 58

A man in Mississippi climbs the steps to a segregated theater section where Black movie-goers had to sit.

INTRODUCTION

The Way It Was

In December 1865, the Thirteenth Amendment to the U.S. Constitution abolished slavery in the United States. By the early 1870s, former slaveholding states in the South created Black codes to strictly limit the freedom of their Black citizens. These restrictions were known as "**Jim Crow**" laws, and they controlled where people who used to be enslaved could live and work.

Jim Crow laws were expanded in the 1880s to keep Black citizens from voting or receiving a proper education. In many parts of the South, they were forced to use separate restaurants, schools, restrooms, parks, and other public places. This practice is known as **segregation**. Although laws said that these spaces should be "separate but equal," facilities for Black people were almost always inferior to those assigned to white citizens.

It was not uncommon for Black citizens in the South to be kidnapped and beaten, shot, or killed for small violations of Jim Crow laws. **Lynchings** and white mob violence frequently terrorized many Black communities. Black churches were burned down, and Black homes attacked. **Discrimination** against Black Americans also existed in the North and elsewhere in the nation, but less so than in the South at the time.

Fighting Back

Segregation, Jim Crow laws, and discrimination denied Black Americans the same **civil rights** as white Americans. In the face of **oppression** and terror, some Black Americans organized to fight inequality. The first civil rights organization in the United States was founded in 1896 as the National Association of Colored Women's Clubs. In 1909, an interracial group of **activists** formed the National Association for the Advancement of Colored People (NAACP). The NAACP called for an end to segregation in schools, public transportation, and other areas of daily life. The group also focused on making the American public aware of the violence against Black people.

In the following years, new civil rights groups emerged. Christian ministers, African American lawyers, and Black youth were especially important in organizing and supporting the emerging civil rights movement. The decade between 1955 and 1965 would serve as the heart of the movement, as action and long-awaited progress began to take shape.

Students in Greensboro, North Carolina, spark the country's youth into peaceful protest.

1960

This book recounts how **sit-ins** reached their peak in 1960 as students in Greensboro, North Carolina, and Nashville, Tennessee, called the nation's attention to what could be accomplished through peaceful protest. **Desegregating** interstate public transportation would also become a goal for activists. A case heading to the U.S. Supreme Court that fall, to be argued by civil rights lawyer Thurgood Marshall, was instrumental to that plan. Finally, the ongoing effort to **integrate** schools as ordered by *Brown v. Board of Education of Topeka,* and *Brown II* exploded in more violence when Ruby Bridges and three other first graders became a symbol of what the future would look like. More and more, students were becoming the most passionate fighters in the struggle for equality. ■

Four Black students refused to leave this whites-only lunch counter in Greensboro.

1

Four Freshmen Sit Down

On Monday, February 1, 1960, four Black teenagers took a stand against restaurant segregation by sitting down at a whites-only lunch counter in Greensboro, North Carolina. Refusing to leave until they were served, these students could no longer accept the discrimination they had experienced since childhood.

The sit-in came after months of discussion between Joseph McNeil, David Richmond, Ezell Blair Jr. (now known as Jibreel Khazan), and Franklin McCain. They were all freshmen at North Carolina Agricultural and Technical State University, a historically Black school in Greensboro. Students at a nearby historically Black women's school called Bennett College had been strategizing a sit-in for months. The young

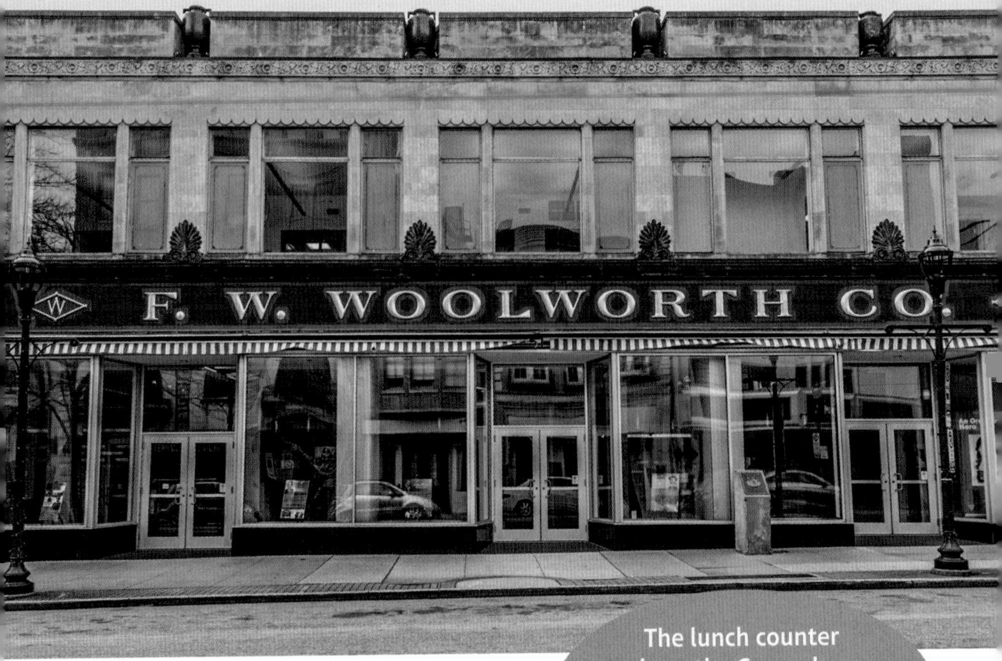

The lunch counter where the Greensboro sit-ins began was inside this Woolworth's, a popular retail store.

men had attended their meetings, although a plan of action had not yet been decided on.

Everything changed during Christmas break. McNeil visited New York, where most of its citizens treated him as an equal. He liked the way that felt. His bus ride back to Greensboro included a rest stop in Richmond, Virginia. When McNeil ordered a burger at the station lunch counter, he was denied service. The discrimination hit him hard, as did a realization: something *must* be done about segregation. *Now.*

Back at school, McNeil, Richmond, Blair, and McCain came up with a plan and a date. The night before, they stayed up talking. They were nervous. The next day could lead to arrest—or death.

The four young men walked from campus to town. Three wore their best clothing, and Franklin wore his Air Force **ROTC** uniform. They stopped to tell Ralph Johns, a white store owner who opposed segregation, what they were doing. Johns promised to call the press.

At about 4 p.m., the four students entered the F. W. Woolworth department store, where Black people were allowed to shop, but not to eat. Purchasing toothpaste and a few other items, they clutched their receipts, exchanged nods, and sat on four of the lunch counter's shiny metal swivel stools with colorful cushions. Politely, they ordered coffee.

Refused service, they showed their receipts—they had just been served a few feet away. The waitress pointed to the snack area at the far end of the counter. It had no seats. Blacks could order there, but they had to either eat standing up or take their food to go.

Franklin McCain (left) and David Richmond, two of the Greensboro Four college students.

A monument on the North Carolina A&T campus depicts the Greensboro Four leaving Woolworth's on February 1, 1960.

The four stayed put. They did not know what would happen, but the act of sitting in those seats gave each of them a rush of pride and worth so great that none of them cared.

The manager asked them to leave and then called the police. An officer arrived and paced behind them, pounding his club into his palm. The students' hearts raced, but they did not flinch. The officer finally left—there was nothing he could do because the four were not breaking any laws.

Woolworth's lunch counter closed at 5:30 p.m., and the men stood to leave. A reporter showed up in time to photograph them walking out. They would soon be known as the Greensboro Four.

The First Sit-In

Eighteen years before the Greensboro Four, a coffee shop in Chicago, Illinois, was the site of the first sit-in.

In 1942, James Farmer, a young Black man, wanted to buy a donut at Jack Spratt's. The man behind the counter wanted to charge him a dollar for a donut that cost white people a nickel.

Farmer had studied the principles of activist Mohandas Gandhi, who had used **nonviolent resistance** during India's struggle for independence. He saw how they had created change in that nation. He decided to put this belief into practice.

Farmer left and returned to Jack Spratt's with some friends. They demanded to be served and to be charged the same prices as the shop's white customers. The police responded to the manager's call but could not make arrests since the demonstrators were nonviolent. Finally, Farmer and his friends were allowed to purchase their breakfast at the same prices offered to white customers.

Determined to end segregation nonviolently, James Farmer cofounded and directed the Congress of Racial Equality (CORE).

A Movement Ignites

The next day, the four students returned at 11 a.m. with about 20 other students, including some women. They ordered lunch, but were refused service. The students would not leave and sat at the counter doing schoolwork until 3 p.m. while white customers **harassed** them. The press arrived, and the sit-in made the evening news.

The following day brought more than 60 protesters from several schools. At least one third of them were women, many from Bennett College. They were met with more white opposition—including members of the **Ku Klux Klan** (KKK).

Joseph McNeil (from left), Franklin McCain, Billy Smith, and Clarence Henderson at the Woolworth's lunch counter on the second day of the sit-in.

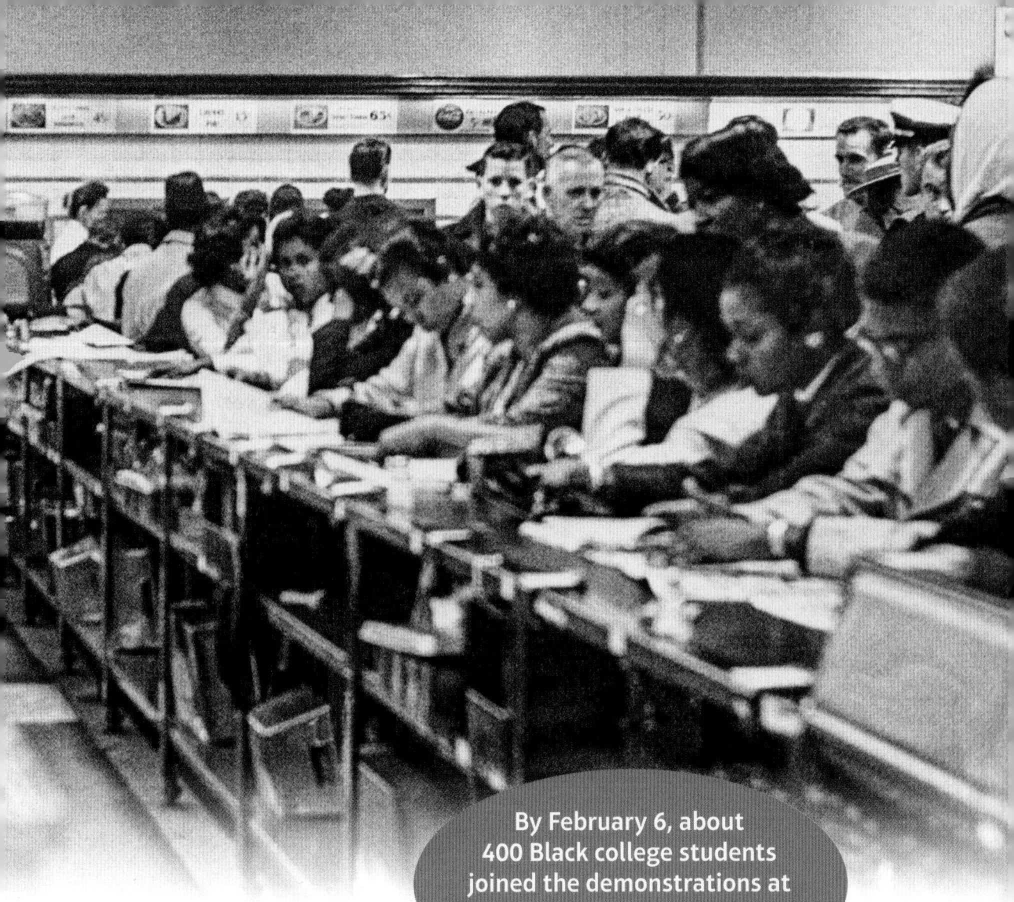

The crowd yelled insults and threatened the students with violence.

More than 300 students piled into Woolworth's on February 4, filling not only the lunch counter but the entire store. Some of them headed to a second lunch counter in town at a store called S. H. Kress & Co.

With each day, the sit-ins grew in strength. News spread, inspiring students elsewhere to act. Within days, sit-ins were happening across North Carolina. Within weeks they had reached Virginia and South Carolina.

Nashville student demonstrators including John Lewis (center in light suit) are hustled to jail after being attacked by a white mob during a sit-in.

Nashville Sit-Ins

When news of the Greensboro Four reached Nashville, Tennessee, student activists Diane Nash and John Lewis, members of the Nashville Student Movement, knew it was time to act. On February 13, at about 12:30 p.m., 129 mostly Black students from several colleges entered three stores in Nashville and requested service at the lunch counters. Refused, they stayed for two hours before leaving. The Nashville sit-ins quickly grew in size, with hundreds of students participating. They were often assaulted by white youths, who poured ketchup and mustard over their heads and threw lit cigarettes on them.

For more than a year, however, this well-organized group had been trained in nonviolent strategies by the Nashville Christian Leadership Council (NCLC). The NCLC was a branch of the Southern Christian Leadership Conference (SCLC), which was headed by the Reverend Dr. Martin Luther King, Jr. A local pastor and student, James Lawson, ran these training workshops in his church basement. As James Farmer had done, he modeled them after the teachings of Mohandas Gandhi. Participants pledged to remain peaceful even when their lives were threatened.

The Reverend James Lawson runs a meeting about lunch counter integration.

A white youth joins Black demonstrators on February 27. Moments later, he would be yanked from his chair and beaten by white attackers.

No Justice

On February 27, violence erupted in Nashville. White crowds at three downtown stores where sit-ins were taking place attacked protesters. At McClellan's store, a white man angry with the students sitting in, knocked a white protester from his chair and beat him. One Black man was shoved down a flight of stairs. These students never fought back. Police arrived and began arresting the protesters as their attackers went free. Soon police began arresting the Black youth demonstrators at the Woolworth's next door. By the afternoon, 82 protesters (77 Black and five white) had been arrested in Nashville while a white mob cheered. The police couldn't arrest any more students—the jail was full. Found guilty in court and offered $50 bail, most of the protesters refused it: they chose jail time over paying a fine. They wanted to make discrimination costly. Housing prisoners cost the local government money, and paying fines would support the injustice of their arrests. These arrests brought national media coverage—and more arrests would follow. Some demonstrators brought toothbrushes along for every protest, anticipating being arrested and jailed.

James Lawson is arrested for training Nashville students in nonviolent protest.

On February 29, thousands of spectators wait outside the Nashville courthouse, where 82 student protesters are convicted after a one-day trial.

The Nashville students' disciplined approach to nonviolent resistance and their written code of conduct became models for the expanding sit-in movement. Several of them would become leaders in the civil rights movement, including Nash, Lewis, and Bernard Lafayette—all of whom would be arrested dozens of times. Lawson was arrested for **inciting** the sit-ins and **expelled** from school. ■

In 1993, the Woolworth's store in downtown Greensboro, which had been open since 1939, closed its doors for good. The company planned to demolish the building.

Greensboro radio station 102 JAMZ started a campaign to save the historic building where the sit-in movement had begun. The station broadcast in front of the empty storefront day and night to save the site. Eighteen thousand people signed a **petition,** including civil rights leader the Reverend Jesse Jackson. Three days after the radio station began its campaign, the F. W. Woolworth company announced an agreement to keep the building standing while its sale could be arranged.

The former Woolworth's store would eventually become home to the International Civil Rights Center and Museum. Fifty years to the day after the sit-ins began in Greensboro, the museum opened. Part of the original lunch counter is housed inside; another part is in the Smithsonian Institution in Washington, DC.

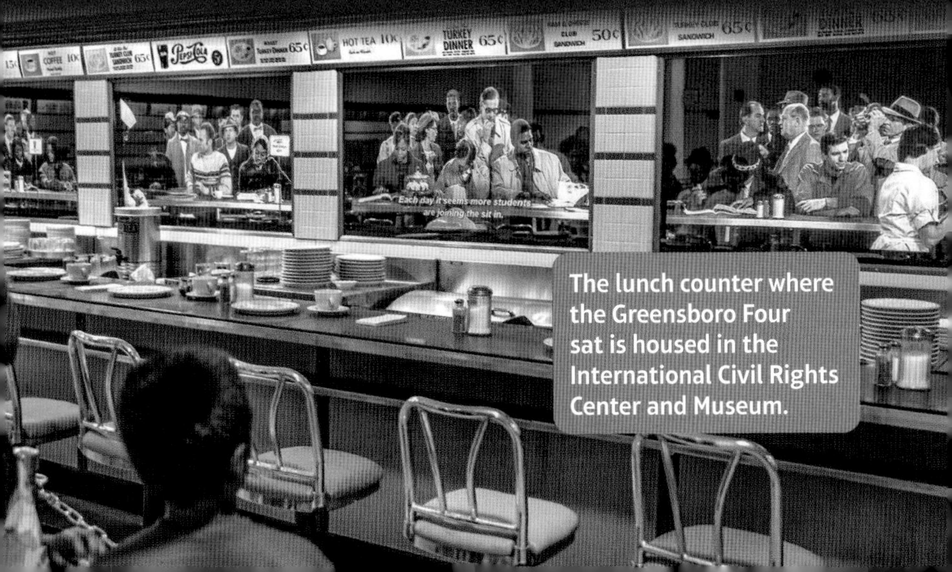

The lunch counter where the Greensboro Four sat is housed in the International Civil Rights Center and Museum.

Children were trained in nonviolent protest. They were taught to put up with the type of harassment they were likely to face at sit-ins.

2

Springing into Action

While the sit-in movement was pushing desegregation in restaurants, segregationists were resisting attempts to create educational change. **Federal** judge J. Skelly Wright of the Eastern District of Louisiana remained determined to desegregate public schools, but Louisiana governor Jimmie Davis and the state **legislature** continued to resist. So did local elected officials, such as Mayor deLesseps Morrison of New Orleans, and a **white supremacy** organization called the Citizens' Council of Greater New Orleans. This hate group distributed racist flyers designed to encourage white parents to fight against the desegregation of their children's schools.

Tensions in New Orleans mounted. The Orleans Parish School Board asked Judge Wright for an

Judge J. Skelly Wright insisted on desegregating the Orleans Parish public schools.

extension of his March 1 deadline to create a desegregation plan for New Orleans schools. He gave them until March 16.

The school board failed to meet Wright's latest deadline. Frustrated by the city's **defiance** of federal law, the judge made his own plan. Beginning in September, children could transfer to any public school in the city, and their parents could choose any of the former white or Black schools closest to their home. He decided that the initial integration would apply only to the first grade, which carried the highest percentage of Black students.

Sharpeville Massacre

In 1960, South Africa had a legal form of segregation called **apartheid**, by which Black residents were subject to different laws than white people. On March 21, Black residents were protesting South African pass laws, which required citizens to carry pass books, papers explaining their identity, address, and place of employment. These pass books supported discrimination by controlling where Black citizens went.

Between 5,000 and 10,000 demonstrators arrived at the police station, intending to peacefully surrender themselves to be arrested for not carrying their pass books. As the crowd grew, the police presence increased. Although the protesters were not armed, police began firing into the crowd. Sixty-nine people were killed, including 10 children. 189 people were injured.

On March 21, 2002, Nelson Mandela, the first Black president of South Africa, opened a memorial to the victims of Sharpeville.

In 1970, a 10th anniversary commemoration of the Sharpeville Massacre included a reenactment.

Students Take the Lead

In April, the Civil Rights Act of 1960 passed in the Senate and headed for President Dwight D. Eisenhower's approval. The act was an effort to increase voter protections for Black people. Unfortunately, the new bill failed to provide stricter guidelines for integrating public education—an area where the Civil Rights Act of 1957 had also fallen short.

Motivated by the need for more action, Ella Baker, the executive director of the SCLC, convened a Youth Leadership Conference at Shaw University in North Carolina. She believed that integration could be achieved more quickly if student groups throughout the South united.

Ella Baker's nickname was the Swahili word "Fundi." It means a person who passes a craft to the next generation.

Black students in Florida hold a peaceful demonstration for civil rights.

Baker was able to use $800 of the SCLC's small treasury to fund the event. She and Dr. King both signed a call to action, inviting young people to attend the conference. This invitation was sent out to 56 institutions of higher education and 58 communities across the South.

Overcoming Injustice

Dr. Martin Luther King, Jr., had become such a powerful force in the civil rights movement that southern officials were determined to discredit and silence him. Early in 1960, the state of Alabama had charged him with signing false tax returns, a crime that would carry a long prison sentence. Soon after, a group of celebrities who were supporters of King formed the Committee to Defend Martin Luther King and the Struggle for Freedom in the South. In early March, they issued a press release opposing the charges.

On March 29, the *New York Times* ran a full-page fund-raising advertisement for the committee. Signed by 64 people, including former First Lady Eleanor Roosevelt and actor Marlon Brando, the ad, titled "Heed Their Rising Voices," detailed what southern officials had been doing to oppress King, student protesters, and all Black southern citizens.

The *New York Times* was sued by an Alabama government official who said this ad made false statements against him. The Supreme Court ruled in the newspaper's favor.

In May, King was acquitted of all charges by an all-white jury.

Dr. King (center) poses with members of the newly formed SNCC.

On Easter weekend, 126 student sit-in leaders from 12 states met in Raleigh. They were joined by students from other organizations: CORE, the Fellowship of Reconciliation, the National Student Association, and the Students for a Democratic Society.

At the gathering, student sit-in leaders decided to form their own organization rather than join with an established civil rights group. It would be called the Student Nonviolent Coordinating Committee (SNCC). Baker acted as their **mentor** and adviser.

Baker told the attendees that their experiences made them their own strong leaders. SNCC would be a democracy, with each local group making its own policies and decisions. She felt that the people out there doing the work should decide the agenda for the organization.

Young female activists waiting in the city jail after being arrested at the Atlanta, Georgia, sit-ins on March 15.

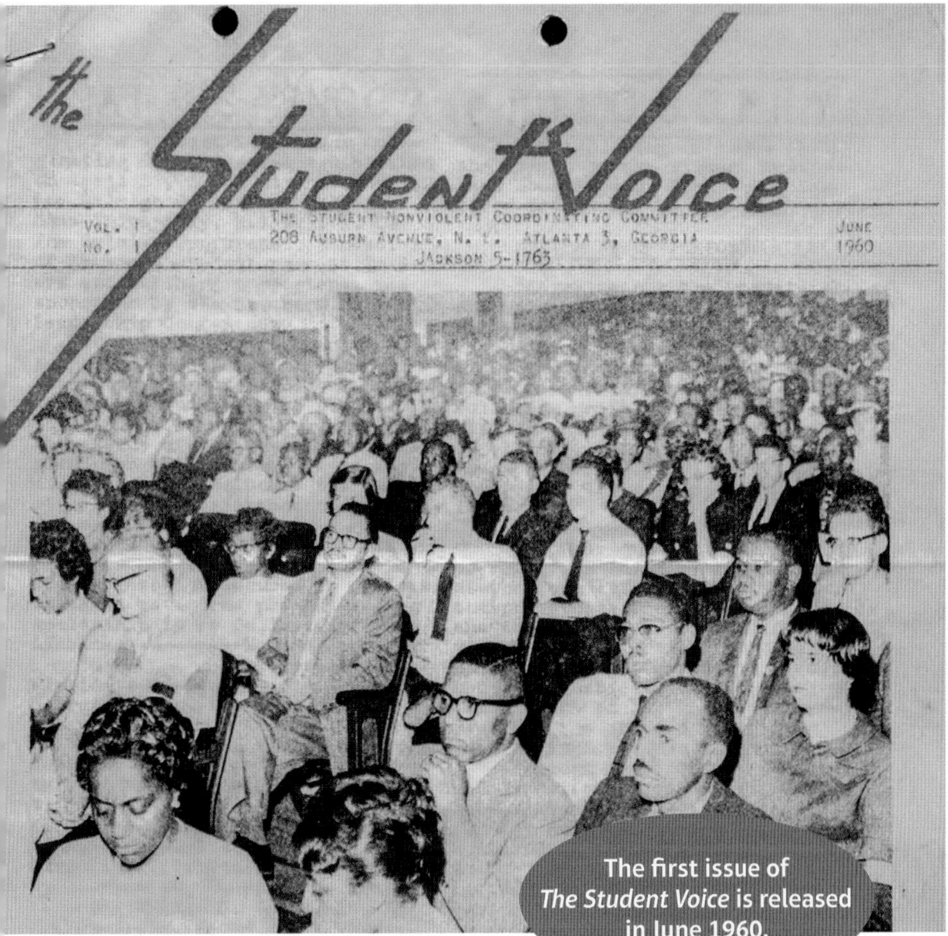

The first issue of *The Student Voice* is released in June 1960.

Local groups established their own SNCC offices. Diane Nash, John Lewis, and Bernard Lafayette were among the members of the Nashville Student Movement who joined. So did their mentor, James Lawson. Soon, a member newsletter would be established: *The Student Voice.*

During the weekend, the young people shared their struggles and made future plans. One new idea was to hold "kneel-ins"—kneeling in prayer outside

At this Jackson, Mississippi, lunch counter, protesters are subjected to vicious attacks.

Sit-Ins Across the Nation

- By the end of February 1960, there were sit-ins in more than 30 communities in seven states.
- By March 1960, 1,000 Black protesters had been arrested at sit-ins.
- On March 16, San Antonio, Texas, became the first southern city to desegregate lunch counters.
- During the spring of 1960, sit-ins took place in 55 cities in 13 states.
- By the end of April, sit-ins had reached every southern state.

whites-only churches. These kneel-ins would have a profound effect on ministers. Within months, the leaders of the United Presbyterian Church would declare that laws upholding racial discrimination were serious violations of the laws of God.

A major question among the students was whether to maintain the principle of nonviolence in their protests. The Nashville members insisted that nonviolent resistance must be continued. Their argument would be continually challenged by other SNCC members who wanted to fight back. ■

Sit-in training included how to withstand many kinds of assault.

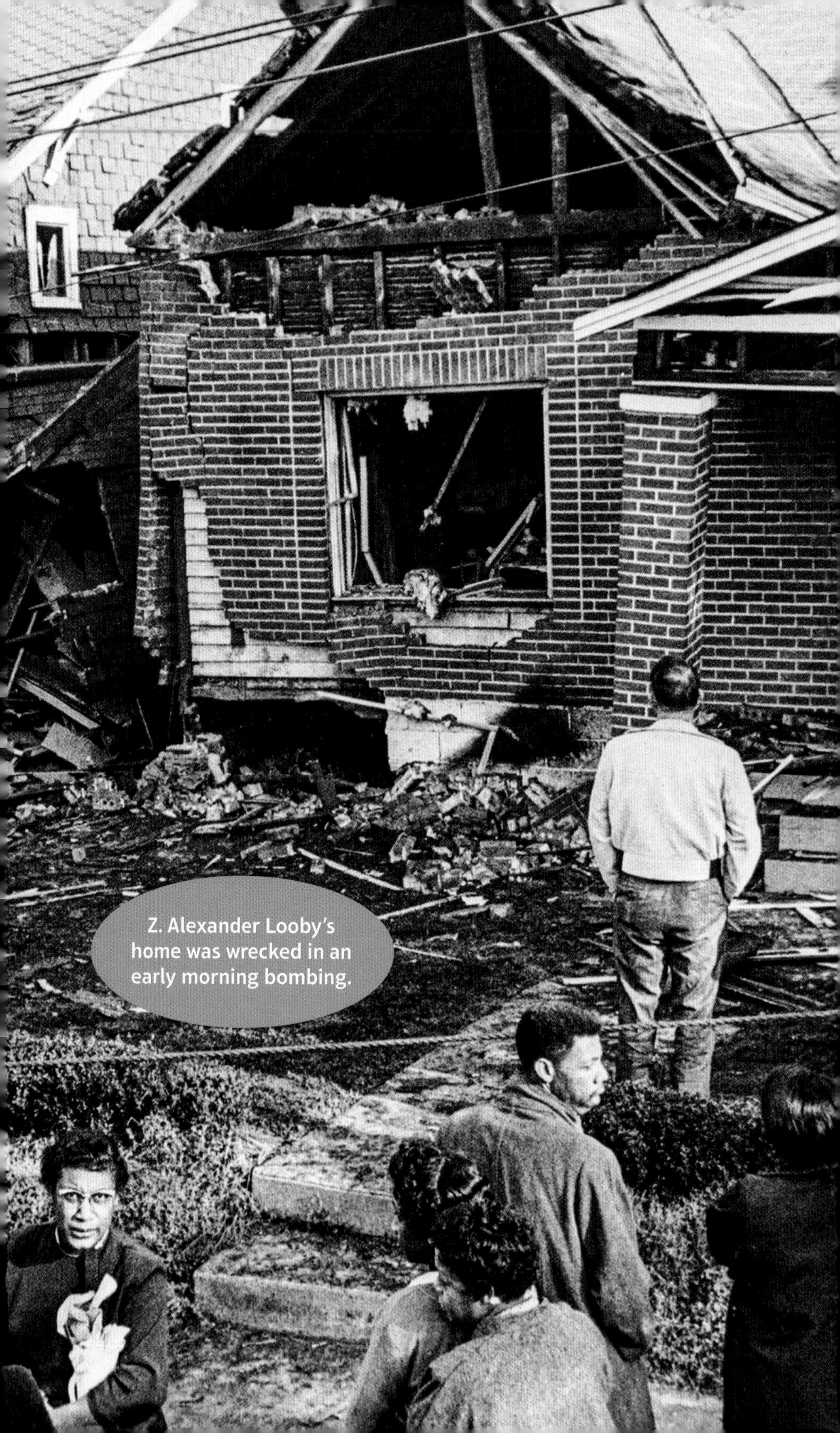

Z. Alexander Looby's home was wrecked in an early morning bombing.

3

Victory and Setbacks

On April 19, 1960, a bomb destroyed the home of Z. Alexander Looby, one of the Black attorneys who had represented the Nashville students arrested at the sit-ins. Miraculously, Looby and his family escaped unharmed.

In response to this attack, sit-in students and Black religious leaders marched to the steps of Nashville's City Hall, where they were met by Mayor Ben West. Diane Nash asked West if he thought discrimination was wrong. Previously, West had freed students serving time in jail for the sit-ins—but he had stopped short of a public statement. On this day, his public admission that discrimination *was* wrong turned the tide against lunch counter segregation.

The bombing of Looby's home sends protesters marching toward Nashville's City Hall.

Negotiation Leads to Victory

West arranged secret meetings between leaders of the Nashville sit-ins and local merchants to desegregate lunch counters. During the first week of May, they reached an agreement.

That same week, President Eisenhower signed the Civil Rights Act of 1960 into law. When he had proposed this act to Congress the year before, he had intended to address and protect all civil rights—and he wanted to legally end racial discrimination in the South. But southern lawmakers in Congress fought against Eisenhower's wishes. The president was forced to remove parts of the bill that provided enforcement practices for integrating schools. By the time the act passed in Congress, it focused primarily on voting rights, but even these protections were not significant and failed to provide effective penalties for cities and towns that systematically **suppressed** Black voters. Many other discriminatory practices remained unaddressed, such as segregation in restaurants, schools, and public transportation.

The Civil Rights Act of 1960 is signed into law by President Eisenhower.

Diane Nash (second from right) and fellow students eat lunch at Nashville's newly desegregated bus terminal.

The students of Nashville accomplished what Eisenhower did not. On May 10, 1960, six downtown stores quietly opened their lunch counters to Black customers. As arranged, Black diners arrived in groups of two or three throughout the afternoon. There were no problems. Nashville had become the first major southern city to integrate its lunch counters.

Feeling the Heat

When summer came, things heated up politically in the United States. Eisenhower's second term was ending, and there were two candidates for the presidency: Republican vice president Richard Nixon and Democratic senator John F. Kennedy from Massachusetts. Dr. King did not think either candidate had shown support for civil rights. On July 10, the night before the Democratic National Convention, members of the NAACP rallied outside the convention site in Los Angeles, California. When Kennedy spoke to the protesters, he received boos because he had not always voted in the Senate in favor of civil rights. He would have to *prove* he supported civil rights if he wanted to win over the Black vote in this tight presidential race.

Senator Kennedy reviews a speech with members of the NAACP during the Democratic National Convention.

Victory in Greensboro

The sit-in movement waged on: students wouldn't quit until they achieved desegregation. In Greensboro, five months after the first sit-in sparked the movement, victory was on the menu at Woolworth's. The store had suffered nearly $200,000 in losses (more than one million dollars today), and the store manager had his salary reduced for not meeting sales goals. On July 25, he asked four Black employees, Geneva Tisdale, Susie Morrison, Anetha Jones, and Charles Bess, to change out of their work clothes and sit at the counter. The four ordered meals. Segregation was over at Woolworth's, and the rest of the Greensboro stores followed.

Charles Bess was in his early twenties, working as a busboy at Woolworth's, when the Greensboro Four sat down.

A scene from the film *To Kill a Mockingbird*, Harper Lee's story of racism in the South.

Fiction Examining Racism

Harper Lee's classic American novel *To Kill a Mockingbird* was published on July 11, 1960. It became an immediate success, winning Lee critical acclaim and a Pulitzer Prize the next year.

The novel, narrated by a young white girl named Scout who witnesses racial injustice, was based on Lee's experiences growing up amid segregation in a small southern Alabama town. In the story, a falsely accused Black man goes on trial. He is defended by the narrator's father, Atticus Finch, who is considered to be a moral hero. The book became an Academy Award–winning movie. It is read in most American high schools to this day.

Ax Handle Saturday

In other places, the struggle was far from over. On Saturday, August 27, more than 80 teenagers agreed to sit in at the lunch counter in the W. T. Grant department store in Jacksonville, Florida. They were members of the Jacksonville Youth Council of the NAACP. Sit-ins at different lunch counters around the city had been ongoing the week prior to this Saturday.

A peaceful Jacksonville sit-in is about to erupt into violence.

Segregationists in Jacksonville, Florida, mob the sidewalks while police look on.

White citizens of Jacksonville were riled up and angry. When the managers of the department store decided to close the store early that day, a mob was waiting for the Black protesters. As they left, they were attacked by about 200 white men and boys. First an organized crowd of KKK supporters yelled racial **slurs** at the peaceful demonstrators. Then, failing to get a reaction, they beat the students with wooden ax handles and baseball bats.

The violence against Black people escalates as white mobs grow on Ax Handle Saturday.

The violence escalated. Black passersby were chased by white mobs and beaten in the streets. Jacksonville police stood by, letting it all happen—until a Black street gang jumped in to try to protect the demonstrators. After that, the police assisted the Klan members, hitting anyone Black in sight.

Covered in blood, the Black victims ran to a church for safety. They prayed and sang together, refusing to let their spirits be destroyed. The mob

outside finally left. The next day, the battered students began to plan for a Black **boycott** of local merchants.

The horrific day came to be called Ax Handle Saturday by the national media. However, coverage of the riots in the Jacksonville newspapers was suppressed. Owners of the newspapers did not want the news to reflect poorly on their city and have a negative effect on local businesses. ■

Demonstrators in Atlanta, Georgia, protest racism and discrimination.

4

Taking a Stand

On October 12, 1960, Bruce Boynton's **appeal** finally reached the U.S. Supreme Court. It had been nearly two years since Boynton was convicted of entering a whites-only area in a restaurant at a bus station in Virginia. His lawyer, Thurgood Marshall, had fought the conviction up through the federal courts, and it was upheld every time. Citing constitutional violations in the conviction, Marshall kept filing appeals. His argument was that because Boynton was an interstate traveler, his rights were protected under the Interstate Commerce Act, passed in 1887, and the equal protection clause of the Fourteenth Amendment. This was Boynton's last chance. The decision of the Court's nine justices would not be made for two months, during which time they listened to arguments that would either solidify desegregation in interstate transportation or deal a devastating blow to civil rights.

Dr. King and students are surrounded by Police Captain R.E. Little (left) and two white detectives after leaving Rich's department store.

King Helps in Atlanta

During the spring and early fall, sit-ins had continued in cities across the country. Students from six historically Black colleges in Atlanta, Georgia, however, were not having success negotiating with merchants and city leaders.

They invited Dr. King to join them in a mass sit-in throughout the city on October 19. The students and King were all arrested. After five days, the students were released, but King was ordered to serve four months in prison. He would be put on a prison road crew to work on highways. These crews were sometimes called "chain gangs" because prisoners were shackled together by their ankles to prevent their escape.

Dr. King and a student protester from Spelman College are driven to jail by Captain Little after being arrested at Rich's department store.

Protesters raising their voices against the arrest of Dr. King are escorted to jail by police.

On October 26, King was brought to Georgia State Prison at Reidsville to begin his sentence. The two presidential candidates both realized that any action they took involving King could make or break their chances of being elected. Nixon decided not to risk turning off white supporters. He remained silent. Kennedy phoned Coretta Scott King, King's wife, and expressed his support and concerns over the arrest.

Let's Twist

American Bandstand was one of the most popular TV shows in 1960. In September, Black singer Chubby Checker made a guest appearance on the show singing "The Twist." The song soon became one of the most popular in the country. The twist also became a revolutionary dance movement by allowing couples the freedom to dance without touching each other.

"The Twist" was declared the biggest hit of the 1960s by *Billboard* magazine. It has also been number one on the all-time greatest hits charts.

Chubby Checker's "The Twist" got rave reviews from young people all over the nation.

Dr. King is welcomed home by his wife, Coretta, on his return from Reidsville State Prison.

A day later, Kennedy's brother and campaign manager, Robert Kennedy, called the judge who had sent King to jail. The judge agreed to release King with a $2,000 bond. King was let go on October 27.

The following day, King's father, who was also a minister, endorsed John F. Kennedy for president during his sermon. Days later, on November 8, Election Day, Kennedy defeated Nixon. Some believe it was the elder King's support that helped secure Kennedy's victory.

Falling Short

Despite gains in desegregating restaurants, in the fall of 1960 there was little progress in school desegregation in many areas of the South, where it remained difficult to enforce. Although Judge Wright had ordered first-grade integration in New Orleans beginning in September, the New Orleans mayor, the Louisiana legislature, and the local school board fought hard against it. Wright was forced once again to delay enforcing his plan until November 14. But he would wait no longer!

White mothers of students at McDonogh No. 19 Elementary School in New Orleans defend segregation.

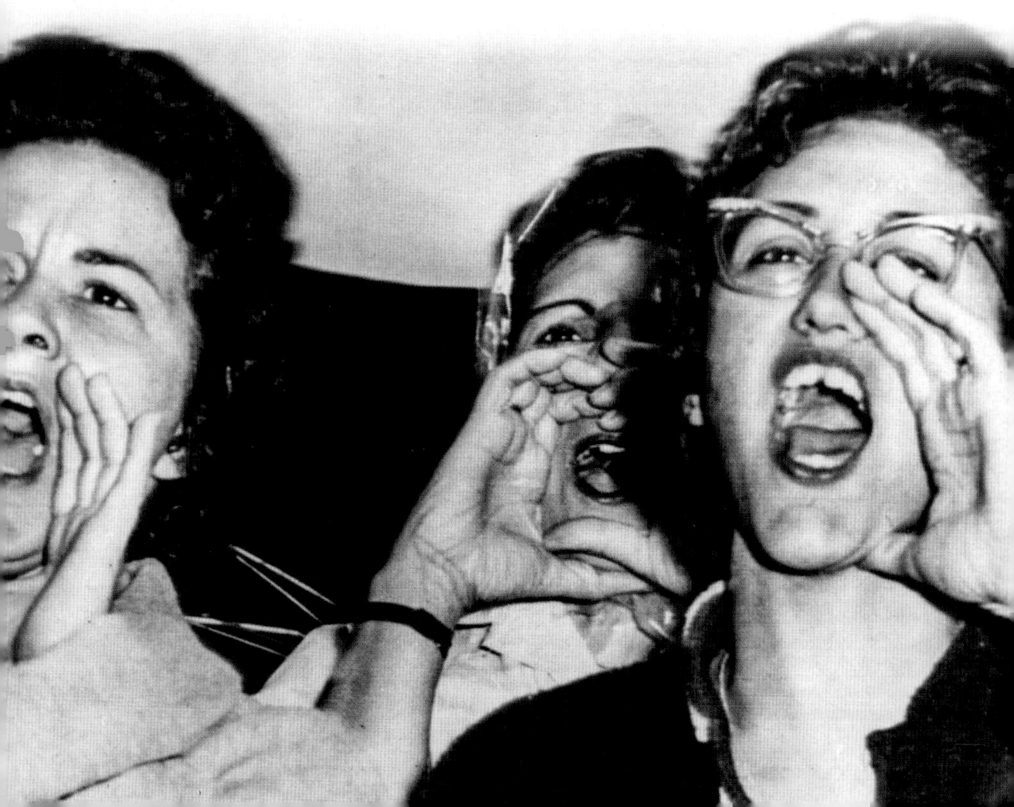

The Greatest

During the 1960 Summer Olympics in Rome, an 18-year-old Black American named Cassius Clay won a gold medal in the light heavyweight division for boxing. Clay immediately turned pro, winning his first match on October 29. In the next three years, he would hold an undefeated record of 19–0 with 15 wins by knockout. At age 22, he won the World Heavyweight Championship in an upset against Sonny Liston. Shortly after, Clay converted to the religion of Islam and changed his name to Muhammad Ali. Known widely for his self-proclaimed nickname "The Greatest," Ali, who died in 2016, is indeed considered one of the greatest boxers of all time.

Cassius Clay becomes a national hero at the Olympics, but back home in Louisville, Kentucky, he is still refused restaurant service.

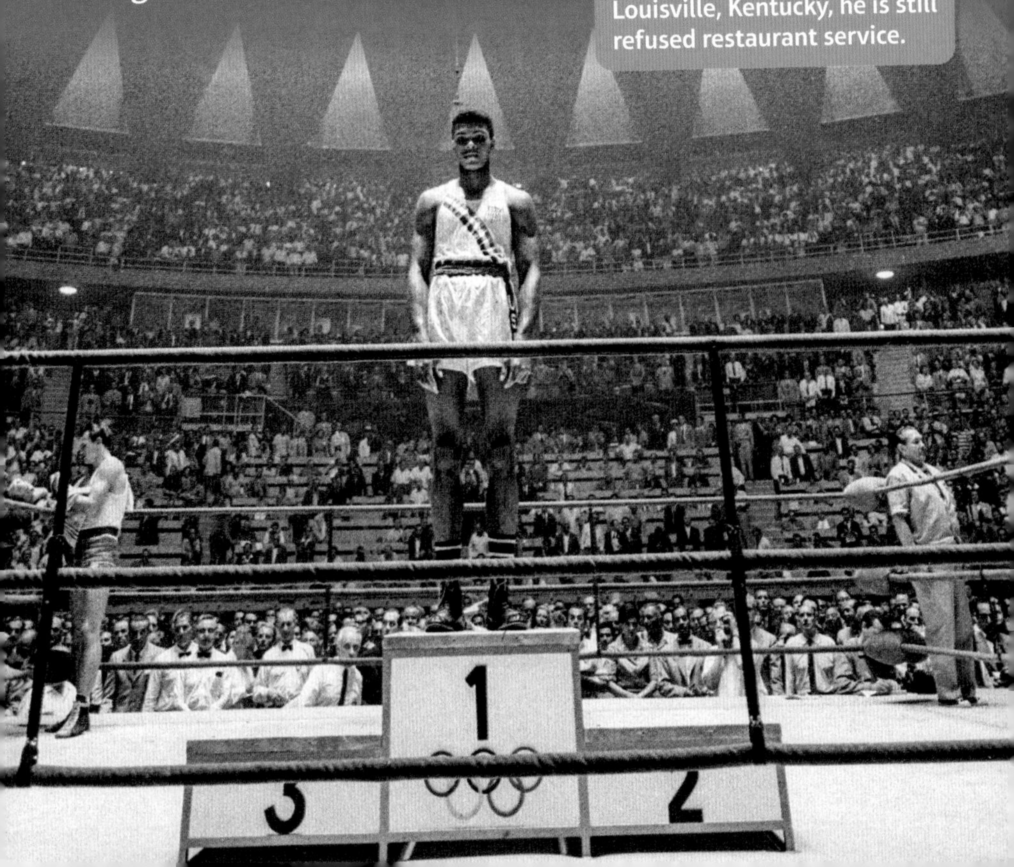

Segregationists carry signs insulting Judge J. Skelly Wright for enforcing the Supreme Court decision to integrate New Orleans public schools.

To make integration even harder, the school board made it difficult for most Black students to change schools. The governor and the legislature tried to block desegregation at the last minute by filing 17 bills that would make it illegal. But the U.S. District Court of Appeals declared all of these bills **unconstitutional** within 24 hours. On November 14, the New Orleans school system was officially desegregated. Four Black six-year-old girls transferred into two formerly

white schools in the Lower Ninth Ward district, a mostly **low-income** area. Though Wright's order had finally been obeyed, the fight against it would turn extremely ugly. ■

A crowd of white teenagers outside the William Frantz Elementary School, in the Lower Ninth district, is dispersed a day after the school is integrated.

Ruby Bridges playing with her friends. As an adult, she wrote a book called *This Is Your Time* to tell children about her experiences.

5

Being the Change

On November 14, 1960, six-year-old Ruby Bridges became the first Black child to attend William Frantz Elementary School in the Lower Ninth district of New Orleans. Ruby and her mother were escorted by federal **marshals** to the school. One of these marshals later recalled that Ruby never cried or whimpered. She marched in like a soldier, and those in her community and those protecting her were proud. Ruby later said that she had no idea that the people yelling and throwing things as she entered school were protesting about her. She thought it was Mardi Gras, a local celebration in which people often behaved that way.

Six-year-olds Leona Tate, Gail Etienne, and Tessie Prevost also transferred to formerly white McDonogh No. 19 Elementary School in the same district in New Orleans. They, too, were escorted by federal marshals through a screaming mob into the building.

As an adult, Tate recalled trying to speak with one of the white students that day. "It was like I was invisible. . . . No response at all. It was like I wasn't even there."

Inside both schools, white parents whisked their children away moments after the girls arrived. A white boycott of the schools began.

On November 16, a riot broke out at the Orleans Parish school board meeting, and the board members who had voted for integration were fired.

A group of white parents on the sidewalk across from McDonogh No. 19 expresses anger about integration at their elementary school.

Ruby Bridges is escorted into school by U.S. marshals for her first three weeks of school.

Although white students slowly returned to William Frantz Elementary, few accepted Ruby's integration, and no first graders would join her class. U.S. marshals continued to protect her. On the way into school one day, a woman threatened to poison Ruby; another woman held up a Black baby doll in a coffin. Because of these threats, Ruby could only eat food she brought from home.

Barbara Henry

All of the teachers at William Frantz Elementary School refused to teach Ruby Bridges, except for one. Twenty-eight-year-old Barbara Henry taught Ruby alone in a classroom for a year, just the same as if all the desks were occupied.

Henry had been educated in a private school that welcomed students of all races. She did not understand how a teacher could refuse to teach any student. Ruby embraced Barbara's caring as much as her lessons. The two created a safe space for the young girl, shutting out the hurt of cruelty and **prejudice** that surrounded them both inside and outside the building.

By standing up against racism and putting her own life at risk, Barbara Henry became a shining light in a dark period of American history. She set an example of love conquering hate, glad to be there for a little girl who needed not only an education, but someone on her side.

Teacher Barbara Henry did not care about the color of Ruby's skin.

Ruby Bridges's parents supported their daughter integrating her elementary school despite the challenges.

Ruby's family was also treated badly by people who opposed integration. Her grandparents were forced to move from the land they had farmed for 25 years. Her father, Abon, lost his job. Some stores refused to sell groceries to the family. At times, Ruby's father thought it would be better to pull her out of the integrated school, but her mother, Lucille, insisted that Ruby should have the better education and opportunities found at William Frantz Elementary.

None of the approximately 200 white students returned to McDonogh No. 19 Elementary. Leona, Gail, and Tessie, called the McDonogh Three, would be the only students in the school for nearly two years. A racist crowd of people chanted against them outside the school every day.

White students and parents gather across the street from McDonogh No. 19 two weeks after it has been integrated.

The three Black first graders leave McDonogh No. 19 the second day after the school is integrated.

Like Ruby, the three girls were guarded by marshals. Classroom windows were covered with brown paper, and the girls had recess in the school theater because the yard was dangerous. The school water fountains were shut off for fear the girls would be poisoned.

Ruby Bridges and President Barack Obama discuss the painting during her visit.

The Problem We All Live With

Popular American artist Norman Rockwell portrayed Ruby Bridges attending school in 1960 as a painting. His imagery shocked the nation because of its honest depiction of her experience. A racial slur is scrawled on the wall behind her, and so are the initials "KKK." A smashed tomato lies nearby. These are just some of the things Ruby had to endure each day as she went to school.

Rockwell's painting first appeared in *Look* magazine in 1964. Previously, Rockwell had been known for his portrayals of American life. However, he wanted to explore themes of social justice in his work.

After the painting was published, Rockwell received stacks of hate mail. He was called a traitor to the white race.

In July 2015, Ruby Bridges visited President Barack Obama in the White House, where he had Rockwell's original painting installed in a hallway outside the Oval Office.

The four little girls who integrated the New Orleans school system would continue to make advancements in civil rights. The McDonogh Three would move to desegregate another New Orleans school in third grade. Today, Leona Tate is working to turn the McDonogh No. 19 school into a museum and learning center to promote civil rights and end racism. She, Etienne, and Prevost are still good friends. Ruby Bridges is still an activist who lives in New Orleans. There is a statue honoring her in the courtyard of William Frantz Elementary. ■

Ruby Bridges also wrote an autobiography called *Through My Eyes* about her experience integrating William Frantz Elementary school.

John Lewis (left) and Bernard Lafayette in a Nashville courtroom after their arrests at a lunch counter sit-in.

6

Supreme Justice

On December 5, 1960, the **verdict** in *Boynton v. Virginia,* the case involving Bruce Boynton, who sat in the whites-only area in a Virginia bus terminal, was announced. The U.S. Supreme Court ruled for Boynton, overturning his conviction and outlawing discrimination in interstate bus terminal facilities nationwide. However, the federal government did little to enforce the ruling.

Bravery on a Bus

Activists John Lewis and Bernard Lafayette were encouraged by the Boynton ruling. They wanted to see it tested. In December, as their school break began, they decided to desegregate a Greyhound bus that was heading out of Nashville to Florida. Instead of sitting in the seats assigned to Black people in the rear of the bus, Lafayette sat behind the driver, and Lewis sat across from Lafayette in the front row. The driver yelled at them to move to the back, but they didn't budge. The disgruntled driver set the bus into motion—heading farther south, where Lewis and Lafayette faced certain danger from violent segregationists.

Bus station segregation is still prominent in this photo from December 1960.

At each stop, the fuming driver stormed off the bus into the station, where he complained to management. Realizing how vulnerable they were, the two young men watched and waited. They kept

their minds off their fear by engaging in conversation. They stayed awake throughout the night.

Deep in the night, they arrived in Troy, Alabama—Lewis's hometown. The local bus stop—a service station—was closed, without so much as a light outside. Here the young men separated. Lafayette faced hours riding by himself down to Florida, but he worried more about Lewis waiting by the road for his ride. Anything could happen in this place where the KKK openly operated. They said goodbye, nervous and fearful of what was to come.

Fortunately, the friends both made it home. And they had desegregated that bus. Just the two of them.

Black men attempt to enter the waiting room and restaurant reserved for white people only in Jackson, Mississippi, in May 1961.

The Reverend Fred J. Shuttlesworth of Birmingham, Alabama, advises students trying to integrate the whites-only waiting room.

A Ride for Freedom

After their triumphant bus trip, Lewis and Lafayette saw an announcement from CORE recruiting volunteers for a Freedom Ride, a bus trip through the South to test enforcement of the Supreme Court ruling to desegregate interstate travel. Both signed up, but Lafayette's parents refused him permission. Lewis joined 12 other activists, six Black and six white, to prepare for the dangerous journey they would take the following spring.

James Farmer (second from left) and other Freedom Riders map out their journey.

Eighteen years after organizing the first restaurant sit-in, James Farmer was now the national director of CORE and the leader of this journey. The 13 activists, known as Freedom Riders, left Washington, D.C., on two public buses—one Greyhound, one Trailways—headed for the Deep South on May 4, 1961. Their ultimate destination was New Orleans; they planned to arrive on May 17 to celebrate the seventh anniversary of the Supreme Court's *Brown v. Board of Education* decision. They had all trained in nonviolent resistance and hoped they could stick with their training even when faced with possible death.

This map traces the route of the bus carrying Freedom Riders out of Montgomery, Alabama.

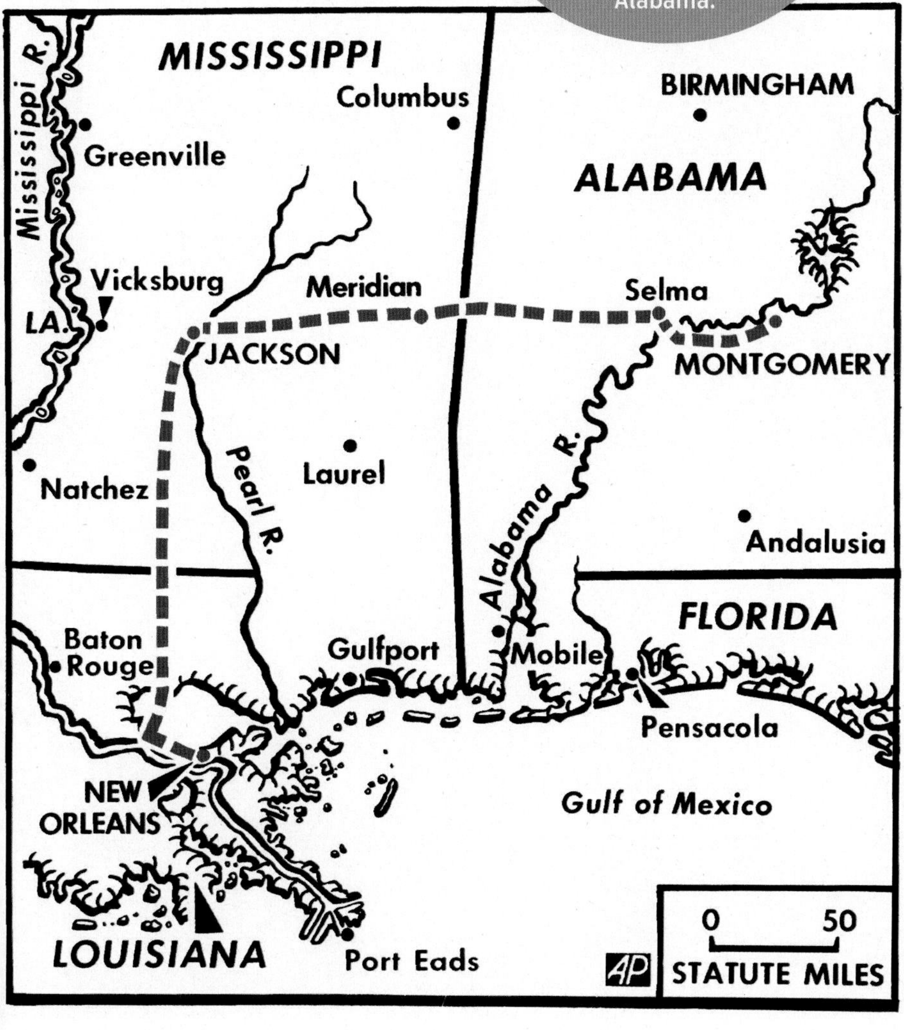

Undercover highway patrol officers were on board to protect the Riders from other passengers. Jim Crow laws about Black people riding in the back of buses in the South were still in effect. However, the Freedom Riders knew they could not guarantee, when the time came, where law enforcement loyalties would lie.

National Guardsmen were posted to buses after Freedom Riders experienced extreme violence in Alabama.

Freedom Riders lift their spirits by singing as they ride in 1961.

The 1961 Freedom Rides would be the first major act of protest in the year ahead. Their impact would be an important **catalyst** propelling the movement toward lasting change for Black Americans across the country. ■

John Fairfield

John Fairfield

John Fairfield was an **abolitionist** who dedicated his life to aiding enslaved people reach freedom. He was an inventive conductor on the **Underground Railroad** until his disappearance in 1860.

Born into a Virginia family of slaveholders, Fairfield believed slavery was evil. His childhood friendship with an African American boy enslaved by John's uncle helped form his views. As young men, the two traveled to Canada so John's friend could live as a free man. Returning home, John discovered that his uncle wanted him arrested. John left and never saw his family again.

Helping reunite freedom seekers with their family and loved ones became Fairfield's mission. His family background gave him the knowledge he needed to pass for a slaveholder and trick owners into giving up people they held in bondage. Fairfield planned elaborate ways to free enslaved people. Once he faked a man's death and then walked the enslaved mourners right out of town to "bury" the deceased—and they kept going until they reached freedom in Canada.

Sometimes Fairfield accepted payment for these missions. He used the money to free other freedom seekers and also support freed men settled in new places. But he was devoted to his calling and would help those who had no means to pay as well.

John Fairfield disappeared just before the Civil War. Historians believe he was killed either while escorting freedom seekers to safety or during a dispute in Tennessee. He was just one of the many Underground Railroad conductors, like Harriet Tubman and Levi Coffin, who led thousands of enslaved people to freedom.

A depiction of enslaved people being led to an Underground Railroad depot.

A sit-in in
Petersburg, Virginia.

CONCLUSION

The Legacy of 1960 in Civil Rights History

What started on February 1, 1960, with four students sitting down for service at a lunch counter had spread to a civil rights revolution. Using the momentum from the success of the sit-ins, students embarked on the Freedom Rides in early 1961, facing unimaginable violence as they worked to desegregate interstate transportation. John Lewis and friends were beaten up in a whites-only waiting room in South Carolina but stayed true to their training in nonviolence. In Anniston, Alabama, police allowed mobs of white people, including KKK members, to attack and set fire to the bus as Freedom Riders barely escaped with their lives. And in Birmingham, the racist Commissioner of Public Safety, Bull Connor, allowed the KKK to brutally attack a group of Freedom Riders for 15 minutes before law enforcement arrived on the scene.

Despite their injuries and the very real possibility of death, the Freedom Riders continued their journey. But with threats mounting and terrified bus drivers refusing to drive them, the leaders of CORE decided that they had achieved their goal of gaining national exposure for civil rights. They elected to fly to New Orleans and safely made it to a rally in celebration of *Brown v. Board of Education* on May 17, 1961. They were greeted by crowds of reporters and shared the details of the vicious hate they had endured. Freedom Rides organized by SNCC continued through the summer of 1961, with new Riders also facing violence and arrest. Finally, in the fall, regulations prohibiting segregation on interstate buses and in terminals were enacted by the Interstate Commerce Commission.

In Alabama, Freedom Riders escape their bus after it has been set on fire by segregationists. Moments later, these Riders were attacked by the white crowd.

A press conference in May 1961 to announce the continuation of the Freedom Rides. John Lewis wears a bandage on his head after being attacked by a white mob.

Many who participated in the events in this book would make names for themselves as civil rights legends, like John Lewis, Ralph Abernathy, and James Farmer. Whether we know their names or not, they are all heroes. Choosing nonviolence, they called attention to what was wrong, and they refused to back down despite danger and hardship.

The threads of desegregation in 1960, restaurant desegregation, interstate public transportation desegregation, and school desegregation, would be woven together, blanketing the civil rights movement with strength, hope, and conviction that America's students were on their way to making America the land of equality for all. ■

James Lawson was a major force in the path toward civil rights.

By mentoring student activists in the principles of nonviolent resistance, James Morris Lawson, Jr., prepared them for the momentous challenges they faced and thus changed the course of the movement.

Born on September 22, 1928, Lawson became a minister like his father and grandfather. He did not believe in violence and war. He refused to serve in the U.S. Army when young American men were

James Lawson received his bachelor of sacred theology degree from Boston University in 1960.

required to do so. He was arrested and convicted for his disobedience, serving 13 months in prison.

Returning to college, Lawson also worked with CORE and the Fellowship of Reconciliation. Both groups believed in nonviolent resistance to racism.

In 1952, he became a missionary in Nagpur, India. There, he studied a type of nonviolent resistance developed by Mohandas Gandhi.

Lawson returned to America and was introduced to Dr. Martin Luther King, Jr., who had also adopted Gandhi's nonviolent beliefs. Under King's influence,

Lawson and the Freedom Riders preferred to risk violence than rely on armed guards during their journey.

Lawson enrolled at Vanderbilt University in Nashville and became a church pastor. He also became the southern director of CORE, as well as working for King's SCLC. He trained students in nonviolent resistance in the church basement.

These students had a goal: they were going to desegregate Nashville lunch counters through sit-in protests. He worked with them for more than a year—until the

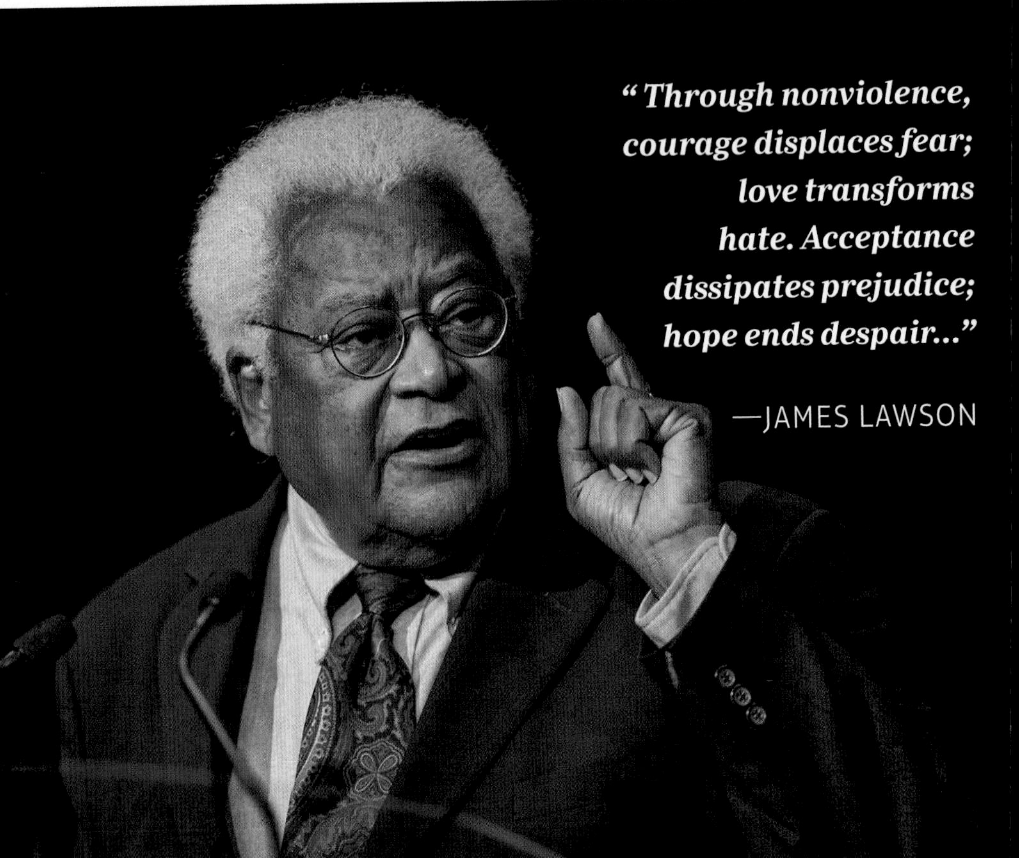

"Through nonviolence, courage displaces fear; love transforms hate. Acceptance dissipates prejudice; hope ends despair..."

—JAMES LAWSON

Greensboro Four started the sit-in movement in July, 1960. His students made him proud—never bowing to the pressure to fight back—enduring pain, indignity, arrest. Lawson was arrested for encouraging the demonstrations. He was expelled from Vanderbilt.

Lawson joined his students in forming SNCC, and he continued to train them. He also trained the Freedom Riders and joined the second wave of Freedom Rides. He was one of 27 Riders arrested and jailed in Jackson, Mississippi. He and the rest of those Riders met with Attorney General Robert F. Kennedy. Soon after, the Interstate Commerce Commission ordered that passengers must be able to sit anywhere on public buses.

In 1962, Lawson moved to Memphis, Tennessee, where he served as a pastor of Centenary United Methodist Church. He remained a pastor for more than fifty years, retiring from the Holman United Methodist Church in Los Angeles in 1999.

Lawson received the Community of Christ International Peace Award in 2004. In 2006, he returned to Vanderbilt University as a professor, after the university apologized for mistreating him. He taught there from 2006 to 2009, and in 2013 he donated his papers to the institution.

Lawson has inspired generations of young people to become activists, including former president Barack Obama.

The Year in Civil Rights
1960

JANUARY 2

Senator John F. Kennedy announces his candidacy for the Democratic presidential nomination.

FEBRUARY 1

Four Black students from North Carolina Agricultural and Technical College sit in at a segregated Woolworth's lunch counter in Greensboro, North Carolina.

FEBRUARY 13

The Nashville Student Movement begins sit-ins. It occupies the Kress, McClellan, and Woolworth's lunch counters in Nashville, Tennessee.

MARCH 16

San Antonio, Texas, becomes the first southern city to desegregate lunch counters.

APRIL 15–17

The Student Nonviolent Coordinating Committee (SNCC) is founded.

MAY 10

Nashville's lunch counters are desegregated.

JULY 25

Greensboro's lunch counters are desegregated.

AUGUST 27

Student protesters in Jacksonville, Florida, are viciously attacked during Ax Handle Saturday.

SEPTEMBER 5

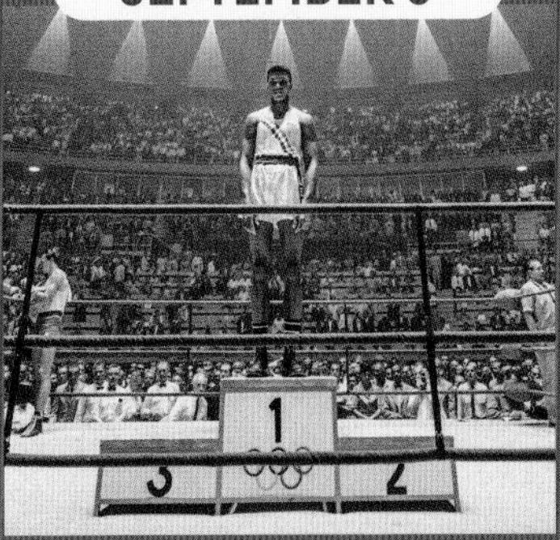

American Cassius Clay wins the gold medal for boxing at the Summer Olympics in Rome.

OCTOBER 19

Dr. Martin Luther King, Jr., is arrested and jailed for 10 days during an Atlanta, Georgia, lunch counter sit-in.

NOVEMBER 14

Amid riots and death threats, Ruby Bridges and three other first-grade girls integrate two New Orleans schools.

DECEMBER 5

In *Boynton v. Virginia,* the Supreme Court declares that segregation in public transportation is illegal in the United States.

GLOSSARY

abolitionist (ab-uh-LISH-uh-nist) someone who worked to abolish slavery before the Civil War

activist (AK-tiv-ist) a person who works to bring about political or social change

apartheid (uh-PAAR-tide) in South Africa, a policy and system of segregation and discrimination on grounds of race

appeal (uh-PEEL) an application to a higher court for a change in a legal decision

boycott (BOI-kaht) a refusal to buy something or do business with someone as a protest

catalyst (KAT-uh-list) a person or thing that causes something to happen

civil rights (SIV-uhl rites) the individual rights that all members of a democratic society have to freedom and equal treatment under the law

defiance (di-FYE-uhns) refusing to obey, or showing an attitude of opposition

desegregate (dee-SEG-ruh-gate) to do away with the practice of separating people of different races in schools, restaurants, and other public places

discrimination (dis-krim-uh-NAY-shuhn) prejudice or unfair behavior to others based on differences in such things as race, gender, or age

expel (ek-SPEL) to make someone leave a school or organization as a punishment

federal (FED-ur-uhl) national government, as opposed to local or state government

harass (huh-RAS) to bother or annoy someone again and again

incite (in-SITE) to stir up feelings that make someone do something violent or foolish

integrate (IN-tuh-grate) to include people of all races

Jim Crow (jim kro) the former practice of segregating Black people in the U.S.

Ku Klux Klan (KOO klux KLAN) a secret organization in the United States that used threats and violence to achieve its goal of white supremacy; also called the Klan or the KKK

legislature (LEJ-uhs-lay-chur) a group of people who have the power to make or change laws for a country or state

low-income (loh IN-kuhm) when a person or family earns or receives a small amount of money, especially from working

lynching (LIN-ching) a sometimes public murder by a group of people, often involving hanging

marshal (MAHR-shuhl) a police officer who is responsible for a particular area

mentor (MEN-tor) a trusted counselor or guide

nonviolent resistance (non-VYE-uh-luhnt ri-ZIS-tuhnce) peaceful demonstration for a political purpose

oppression (uh-PRESH-uhn) the use of power or authority in a cruel and unfair way

petition (puh-TISH-uhn) a letter signed by many people asking those in power to change their policy or actions or explaining how the signers feel about a certain issue or situation

prejudice (PREJ-uh-dis) hatred or unfair treatment that results from having fixed opinions about some group of people

ROTC the Reserve Officers' Training Corps, a program that trains college students for future service in the U.S. military

segregation (seg-ruh-GAY-shun) the practice of keeping groups of people apart based on race or other characteristics

sit-in (SIT-in) a form of protest in which demonstrators occupy a place, refusing to leave until their demands are met

slur (slur) an insult or accusation that is insulting a person's reputation

suppress (suh-PRESS) to put down with authority or force

unconstitutional (uhn-kahn-stuh-TOO-shuh-nuhl) not in keeping with the basic principles or laws set forth in the U.S. Constitution

Underground Railroad (UHN-dur-ground RAYL-rohd) a network of people who secretly helped enslaved people from the South escape to free states in the North or to Canada before the American Civil War

verdict (VUR-dikt) the decision of a jury on whether an accused person is guilty or not guilty

white supremacy (wite su-PREM-uh-see) the belief that the white race is better than other races and that white people should have control over people of other races

BIBLIOGRAPHY

Brimner, Larry Dane. *Twelve Days in May: Freedom Ride 1961.* PA: Calkins Creek Books, 2017.

Chafe, William Henry. *Civilities and Civil Rights: Greensboro, North Carolina, and the Black Struggle for Freedom.* New York: Oxford University Press, 1981.

Fairclough, Adam. *Race and Democracy: The Civil Rights Struggle in Louisiana, 1915–1972.* Athens: University of Georgia Press, 1995.

Houston, Benjamin. *The Nashville Way: Racial Etiquette and the Struggle for Social Justice in a Southern City.* Athens: University of Georgia Press, 2012.

Lafayette, Bernard, Jr. "The First Time John Lewis and I Integrated the Buses." *New York Times*, 2020, nytimes.com/2020/07/18/opinion/john-lewis-dead.html

Levingston, Steven. "John F. Kennedy, Martin Luther King Jr., and the Phone Call That Changed History." *Time*, 2017, time.com/4817240/martin-luther-king-john-kennedy-phone-call

Lewis, John. *Walking with the Wind: A Memoir of the Movement.* New York: Simon & Schuster, 1998.

Walzer, Michael. "A Cup of Coffee and a Seat." *Dissent 7* (Spring 1960): 111–120.

Civil Rights Digital Library, crdl.usg.edu

Civil Rights Movement Archive, crmvet.org

Martin Luther King, Jr. Research and Information Center at Stanford University, kinginstitute.stanford.edu

Nashville Sit-ins, tnmuseum.org

New York Times Archive, nytimes.com/search?query=archives

SNCC Digital Gateway, snccdigital.org

University of North Carolina, Greensboro, libcdm1.uncg.edu

SNCC was devoted to registering every Black voter despite deadly risks.

INDEX

Note: Page numbers in *italics* refer to images and captions.

About the Author

Selene Castrovilla is an acclaimed, award-winning author. Her five books on the American Revolution for young readers include Scholastic's *The Founding Mothers*. Selene has been a meticulous researcher of American history since 2003. She has expanded her exploration into the civil rights movement, as well as the Civil War, in a forthcoming book. A frequent speaker about our nation's evolution, she is equally comfortable with audiences of children and adults. Please visit her at selenecastrovilla.com.

PHOTO CREDITS

Photos ©: cover: Donald Uhrbrock/The LIFE Images Collection/Getty Images; 1: Jack Corn/*The Tennessean*/Imagn Content Services, LLC; 3 top: Bettmann/Getty Images; 3 bottom: Paul Slade/*Paris Match*/Getty Images; 4: Universal History Archive/Universal Images Group/Getty Images; 7: The Granger Collection; 8: Skip Foreman/AP Images; 10: RidingMetaphor/Alamy Images; 11: AP Images; 12: Philip Scalia/Alamy Images; 13: Bettmann/Getty Images; 14: The Granger Collection; 15: Bettmann/Getty Images; 16: Jimmy Ellis/*The Tennessean*/Imagn Content Services, LLC; 17: Donald Uhrbrock/The LIFE Images Collection/Getty Images; 18: Bettmann/Getty Images; 19: Bettmann/Getty Images; 20: Jack Corn/*The Tennessean*/Imagn Content Services, LLC; 21: Lynn Hey/News & Record/AP Images; 22: Howard Sochurek/The LIFE Picture Collection/Getty Images; 24: Richard Tolbert/AP Images; 25: Roger Jackson/Central Press/Hulton Archive/Getty Images; 26: Everett/Shutterstock; 27: Fred E. Noel/AP Images; 28: National Archives and Records Administration; 29: Howard Sochurek/The LIFE Picture Collection/Getty Images; 30: Bettmann/Getty Images; 31: WHS-N71-508/Wisconsin Historical Society; 32: The Granger Collection; 33: Howard Sochurek/The LIFE Picture Collection/Getty Images; 34: Bettmann/Getty Images; 36: Eldred Reaney/*The Tennessean*/Imagn Content Services, LLC; 37: Everett Collection Historical/Alamy Images; 38: Gerald Holly/*The Tennessean*/Imagn Content Services, LLC; 39: Paul Schutzer/The LIFE Picture Collection/Getty Images; 40: Sayaka Matsuoka/Triad City Beat; 41: Moviestore/Shutterstock; 42: Times-Union Archive/USA TODAY NETWORK; 43: Jim Kerlin/AP Images; 44–45: Bettmann/Getty Images; 46: Donald Uhrbrock/The LIFE Images Collection/Getty Images; 48: AP Images; 49: AP Images; 50: Bettmann/Getty Images; 51: AP Images; 52: AP Images; 53: Popperfoto/Getty Images; 54: Marvin E. Newman/*Sports Illustrated*/Getty Images; 55: AP Images; 56–57: AP Images; 58: Paul Slade/*Paris Match*/Getty Images; 60: AP Images; 61: AP Images; 62: Lane Turner/*The Boston Globe*/Getty Images; 63: Paul Slade/*Paris Match*/Getty Images; 64: AP Images; 65: AP Images; 66: White House Photo/Alamy Images; 67: Tyler Kaufman/AP Images; 68: Jack Corn/*The Tennessean*/Imagn Content Services, LLC; 70–71: Ted Russell/The LIFE Picture Collection/Getty Images; 72: Paul Schutzer/The LIFE Picture Collection/Getty Images; 73: AP Images; 74: BHR/AP Images; 75: AP Images; 76: Paul Schutzer/The LIFE Picture Collection/Getty Images; 77: Paul Schutzer/The LIFE Picture Collection/Getty Images; 78: The Granger Collection; 79: Jake Murray; 80: Howard Sochurek/The LIFE Premium Collection/Getty Images; 82: Underwood Archives/UIG/Shutterstock; 83: AP Images; 84–85: Anne Cusack/*Los Angeles Times*/Getty Images; 86 top: Paul Schutzer/The LIFE Picture Collection/Getty Images; 86 bottom: Armondo Arorizo/Prensa Internacional/ZUMPARESS.com/Alamy Images; 87: Bettmann/Getty Images; 88 left: The Granger Collection; 88 top right: Howard Sochurek/The LIFE Picture Collection/Getty Images; 88 bottom right: Gerald Holly/Prensa Internacional/Imagn Content Services, LLC; 89 top left: Bettmann/Getty Images; 89 top right: AP Images; 89 bottom left: Marvin E. Newman/Prensa Internacional/Getty Images; 89 bottom right: AP Images; 93: SBS Eclectic Images/Alamy Images.